# THE LIVING GOSPEL

*Daily Devotions for Advent 2015*

Theresa Rickard, O.P.

AVE MARIA PRESS AVE Notre Dame, Indiana

---

© 2015 by RENEW International

All rights reserved. No part of this book may be used or reproduced in any manner whatsoever, except in the case of reprints in the context of reviews, without written permission from Ave Maria Press®, Inc., P.O. Box 428, Notre Dame, IN 46556, 1-800-282-1865.

Founded in 1865, Ave Maria Press is a ministry of the United States Province of Holy Cross.

www.avemariapress.com

Paperback: ISBN-13 978-1-59471-593-8

E-book: ISBN-13 978-1-59471-594-5

Cover image "Approaching Bethlehem" © 2012 by Jeni Butler, artworkbyjeni.wix.com/art.

Cover and text design by John R. Carson.

Printed and bound in the United States of America.

# Introduction

The word *Advent* comes from the Latin *adventus* and means "the coming" or "showing forth." During the season of Advent, we celebrate the coming of the Savior—in the birth of Jesus and at the end of time. But the season also reminds us to be sensitive to the ways God comes into our lives all year long. The Indian poet Tagore gives us a focus for our Advent prayer and reflection in his poem "Silent Steps": "Have you not heard his silent steps? He comes, comes, ever comes."

I struggle with staying attentive to the present moment—to the everyday. I often find myself distracted, thinking two steps ahead, always in a hurry and trying to accomplish too many tasks at the same time. My daily time of personal prayer helps me to slow down and to once again attune my ear to the Lord's footsteps as he accompanies me each day. Advent reminds me to listen for the Lord's word in the experiences of my life and to remember he is with me—*every moment and every age, every day and every night.*

In the midst of frantic preparation for Christmas, this Advent devotional can help you be attentive and alert to God's silent steps in the midst of your busy life. Prayer and reflection on the daily Mass readings are means of joining the universal Church as together we cry, "Come, O Lord!" The two-page devotion for each day of Advent includes brief prayers, a selection from the gospel reading of the day, a simple reflection, and a call to act on your faith.

I invite you to spend ten minutes with each day's devotion. It is helpful to develop a habit of prayer by choosing the same time and place. I also encourage you to use a bible along with this booklet so that you can read the entire gospel passage for the day. Citations for these are included each day under the heading "Listen." I find it helpful to begin my meditation by listening to a reflective song or instrumental music. It helps me to quiet my mind and settle my restless spirit. Perhaps this will help you too.

Through God's grace and through this Advent devotional, may you become more fully aware of the faithful steps of God as he comes to you *every moment and every age, every day and every night.*

"Come, let us go up to the LORD's mountain,
to the house of the God of Jacob,
That he may instruct us in his ways,
and we may walk in his paths."

*~Isaiah 2:3*

# SUNDAY, NOVEMBER 29
## FIRST WEEK OF ADVENT

BEGIN

*Be still. Be silent. Slowly repeat, "Come, O Lord."*

PRAY

Your ways, O LORD; make known to me;
teach me your paths,
guide me in your truth and teach me,
for you are God my savior,
for you I wait all the day long.

*~Psalm 25:4–5*

LISTEN

*Read Luke 21:25–28, 34–36.*

There will be signs in the sun, the moon, and
the stars, and on earth nations will be in dismay,
perplexed by the roaring of the sea and the waves.
People will die of fright in anticipation of what is
coming upon the world, for the powers of the heav-
ens will be shaken. And then they will see the Son
of Man coming in a cloud with power and great
glory. But when these signs begin to happen, stand
erect and raise your heads, because your redemption is at hand.

*~Luke 21:25–28*

## God's Love Is Stronger than Death

My dad spent more than thirty years as a New York
City police officer, and he was as tender as he was
tough. As he reached old age and his once-strong body

weakened, his mind and indomitable spirit held on. In his last months, he refused to fight against death, and instead he fought for life with a tangible faith and profound confidence in God. He was ninety-two when he died.

Very near the end of his life, on a day when Dad had been mostly unresponsive and we all thought it was the end, my dad suddenly opened his eyes and said, "Hey, Doug, is that you?" My brother-in-law replied, "Yeah, Dad"; with an incredulous look, Dad replied, "Jeez, am I still here?" My brother-in-law called the rest of us, and we joined Dad for a bowl of ice cream. He talked of death as something natural—just another part of living. He died two days later.

Our culture and our instincts would have us flee adversity, but the Gospel reminds us to stand strong. Whether we face the end of time or the end of our lives, when we think we just can't cope anymore, when all seems lost, when God seems to have forgotten us—we may just be closest to our salvation. Christ comes in the hour of our greatest need. Listen for his footsteps. "But when these signs begin to happen, stand erect and raise your heads because your redemption is at hand."

ACT

Send a card or call someone who is facing great adversity. Be the presence of Christ for that friend.

PRAY

Come, O Lord. Heal my anxious heart, help me to stand up and face life and death with faith and courage. Amen.

# Monday, November 30
## First Week of Advent

BEGIN

*Be still. Be silent. Slowly repeat, "Come, O Lord."*

PRAY

I rejoiced because they said to me, "We will go up to the house of the LORD."

*~Psalm 122:1*

LISTEN

*Read Matthew 8:5–11.*

When Jesus entered Capernaum, a centurion approached him and appealed to him, saying, "Lord, my servant is lying at home paralyzed, suffering dreadfully." Jesus said to him, "I will come and cure him." The centurion said in reply, "Lord, I am not worthy to have you enter under my roof; only say the word and my servant will be healed."

*~Matthew 8:5–8*

## God Comes to Heal Us

A number of years ago I was at a parish, giving a talk on the Mass. Afterward, I asked for comments or questions. A woman stood up and said angrily, "I refuse to say the words, 'Lord, I am not worthy.' I have worked so hard rebuilding my self-esteem, and every time I come to Mass I am reminded that I am worthless."

The woman had misunderstood the idea behind that biblical statement. Our admission of our unworthiness before receiving Communion is not meant as a self-indictment; rather, it is an acknowledgment of

Jesus as the power and compassion of God. The focus is on Christ, not us.

The plain truth is that, on our own, we are unworthy to have the Lord come to us, and yet God makes us worthy for that honor and privilege. In the Incarnation, God humbled himself so that humanity could be united to him. That's why Jesus reminds his followers in the Gospel of John, "I no longer call you slaves . . . I have called you friends" (15:15).

In today's gospel reading, Jesus encounters the Roman centurion. The officer begs Jesus to heal his paralyzed servant, saying, "Lord, I am not worthy to have you enter under my roof; only say the word and my servant will be healed." Jesus doesn't respond with the disdain other Jewish people showed to Roman soldiers. Rather, he says to his disciples, "Amen, I say to you, in no one in Israel have I found such faith" (Mt 8:10). Immediately, Jesus' healing spirit enters the home and heart of these "outsiders," healing, saving, and freeing them from every kind of paralysis.

Every day, Christ comes and does for us what he did for the centurion; his healing spirit enters under the roofs of our very souls, setting us free to "go" and be God's healing presence in the world.

ACT

Each time you receive Communion this Advent, pray the words from the Mass with greater attentiveness and ask the Lord for healing: *Lord, I am not worthy that you should enter under my roof, but only say the word and my soul shall be healed.*

PRAY

Come, O Lord. Come into my home and heart this day, and fill me with your healing love. Amen.

# Tuesday, December 1
## First Week of Advent

BEGIN

*Be still. Be silent. Know that God is near.*

PRAY

Justice shall flower in his days, and profound
peace, till the moon be no more.

*~Psalm 72:7*

LISTEN

*Read Luke 10:21–24.*

Jesus rejoiced [in] the Holy Spirit and said, "I give
you praise, Father, Lord of heaven and earth, for
although you have hidden these things from the
wise and the learned you have revealed them to the
childlike."

*~Luke 10:21*

## Tell Me What God Is Like; I'm Starting to Forget

There is a story in *Chicken Soup for the Soul* about a
couple with a four-year-old daughter and a newborn.
The little girl asked to hold her baby brother, and then
told her parents that she wanted to be alone with the
baby. They put her off, hoping she would forget. One
morning, the mother heard the little girl in the baby's
room, talking to her brother. Standing just outside the
room, the mother put her ear to the door and heard the
four-year-old say to the newborn: "Tell me what God
is like, because I am starting to forget."

The innocence of this child and her longing for
God can serve as a great reminder for us to seek God

with a simple and open heart. Jesus reminds us that true wisdom comes from a childlike spirit—one that sees the world and its history as God sees them. We can become so hardened by our disappointments and distracted by our busyness that we fail to remember God and his presence in our lives and in our world. God's desire for us and for our world is one of peace and of humankind flourishing. No matter what is happening in our lives, we must never lose sight of that dream and our hope in the God of love and mercy.

Jesus rejoices in the Holy Spirit because he sees God's imprint everywhere. We have the same capacity to know and recognize God in our daily lives. Every time we experience compassion or show it to another, we know what God is like. At times we can become so numbed by the routine of life and its suffering that we forget who God is, and in turn we forget who and whose we are. When was the last time you experienced real joy? If you can't remember, maybe you are starting to forget what God is like. Come, Lord Jesus, show us the face of God and restore our joy.

ACT

Imagine a person or situation that you are struggling with. Ask God to help you see that person or difficulty through God's eyes. Look for joy in the midst of the struggle.

PRAY

Come, O Lord. Give me a simple and childlike heart so I may remember your presence throughout this day and see everything as you do. Amen.

# WEDNESDAY, DECEMBER 2
## FIRST WEEK OF ADVENT

BEGIN

*Be still. Be silent. Know that God is near.*

PRAY

The Lord is my shepherd, I shall not want.
In verdant pastures he gives me repose;
Beside restful waters he leads me;
he refreshes my soul.

*~Psalm 23:1*

LISTEN

*Read Matthew 15:29–37.*

Great crowds came to Jesus, having with them the
lame, the blind, the deformed, the mute, and many
others. They placed them at his feet, and he cured
them.

*~Matthew 15:30*

## Heal the Wounds

Pope Francis speaks with direct language and poignant imagery. In one of his addresses, he likened the Church to a field hospital or MASH unit for the injured. He said that in this type of hospital, "It is useless to ask a seriously injured person if he has high cholesterol and about the level of his blood sugars. You have to heal his wounds. Then we can talk about everything else." Pope Francis continually speaks about meeting people where they are with the mercy and compassion of God. Jesus—God's mercy and compassion made flesh—excludes no one from his healing love. All are made worthy by his grace.

In today's gospel reading, the crowds gather around Jesus and place their ailing loved ones at his feet. Jesus is moved with compassion and acts. "The crowds were amazed when they saw the mute speaking, the deformed made whole, the lame walking, and the blind able to see, and they glorified the God of Israel" (Mt 15:31). Jesus, who must have been exhausted from the emotional and physical work of healing, became aware of the deep hunger of the crowd. He had empathy for these people who traveled far and sacrificed much to place their loved ones at his feet. He instructed his incredulous disciples to find a way to feed them—and, to the disciples' own amazement, they did.

Jesus healed the sick and fed the hungry. Sometimes we get so caught up in ourselves and our own hurts that we fail to notice the needs of others.

Who in your life needs physical, spiritual, or emotional healing? Place these people at the feet of Jesus. What healing do you need? Place yourself in God's tender arms.

ACT

Pay attention to the people you encounter today. Who is wounded or in need? Find one way to help.

PRAY

Come, O Lord. I place at your feet the people I meet today. Heal them. I place my life before you and ask you to remove all that prevents me from being attentive to their needs. Amen.

BEGIN

*Be still. Be silent. Know that God is near.*

PRAY

Trust in the Lord forever! For the Lord is an eternal Rock.

*~Isaiah 26:4*

LISTEN

*Read Matthew 7:21, 24–27.*

Everyone who listens to these words of mine and acts on them will be like a wise man who built his house on rock. The rain fell, the floods came, and the winds blew and buffeted the house. But it did not collapse; it had been set solidly on rock.

*~Matthew 7:24–25*

## While to That Refuge Clinging

Homes can vary greatly in size, shape, and design, but the need for a solid foundation is the same no matter the type of structure. Your home, or any building, is only as solid and stable as the foundation upon which it is built. The same thing is true of the relationships that form the fabric of our lives.

Jesus exhorts us to be like the wise person who built his house on a rock foundation, and Isaiah reminds us that God is our eternal rock. Here are five steps to strengthen the foundation of your life in order to withstand the storms that threaten your peace and well-being: (1) be firmly rooted in God's

Word by reading it daily, (2) seek God's guidance in every action you take, (3) be aware of God's presence in the events of your day, (4) offer your life to God each morning, and (5) receive the Eucharist regularly.

When a life storm rocks my life and I am feeling anxious and vulnerable, I often sing to myself the Christian hymn "How Can I Keep from Singing." The chorus is:

> No storm can shake my inmost calm
> While to that refuge clinging;
> Since Christ is Lord of heaven and earth,
> How can I keep from singing?

No matter what storm rocks your life, cling to Jesus, who is your refuge and salvation, and keep on singing of the goodness of our God. And when a friend or family member is shaken by life's happenstances, sing this song to them—even if you sing it, like me, a bit off key.

ACT

> According to some human behaviorists, you have to do something twenty-one times for it to become a habit. So, for the rest of Advent, as soon as you wake up each morning, commit your day to God.

PRAY

> Come, O Lord. I cling to you as storms rock my life. You are the rock of my salvation. I offer to you this day, all that I am, and all the activities I undertake. May all these please you. Amen.

# FRIDAY, DECEMBER 4
## FIRST WEEK OF ADVENT

BEGIN

*Be still. Be silent. Know that God is near.*

PRAY

The LORD is my light and my salvation;
whom should I fear?
Wait for the Lord with courage;
be stouthearted, and wait for the LORD.

*~Psalm 27:1, 14*

LISTEN

*Read Matthew 9:27–31.*

As Jesus passed by, two blind men followed him,
crying out, "Son of David, have pity on us!" When
he entered the house, the blind men approached
him and Jesus said to them, "Do you believe I can
do this?" "Yes, Lord," they said to him. Then he
touched their eyes and said, "Let it be done for
you according to your faith." And their eyes were
opened.

*~Matthew 9:27–29*

## Catching Up with Jesus

My friend Mary Ann's Irish mom used to say to her
daughters, "Don't run to catch a train, a bus, or a man,
because there will always be another." In today's gospel reading, two blind men ran to catch up to Jesus
because they knew he was more than just a man. As
he passed by them on the road, they saw Jesus—and I
really mean they *saw* him—and began to follow him.
They caught up to him at his friend's home or, better

said, he caught up to them. He stopped what he was doing and had a faith conversation with them. Jesus asked, "Do you believe?" and they replied, "Yes, Lord, we believe." And their eyes were opened.

Sometimes I am running so fast I lose sight of myself—I have to catch up with me in order to see. When I lose track of myself, I also lose track of God. And when that happens, those with whom I interact every day do not encounter my best self. I become distracted and sometimes a bit cranky. I find that the only way to catch up to God and me is to stop—to stand still. It is in the stillness that God can catch up to us and bring our lives back into peaceful order.

Jesus asked the two blind men, "Do you believe I can do this?" And they replied, "Yes, Lord." So Jesus asks you, "Do you believe?" Are you willing to stand still long enough for Jesus to catch up to you? Do you really want to see? Facing God and yourself is not always easy, but it is the only way to peace.

ACT

Spend ten minutes in silent stillness today and let God catch up with you. Focus on what truly matters, and structure your day around those priorities. Let God's tender kindness lead you.

PRAY

Come, O Lord. Help me to stand still, and give me the grace to quiet the noise in my head and the restlessness of my spirit. Catch up to me, Lord, and restore my calm. Amen.

# Saturday, December 5
## First Week of Advent

BEGIN

*Be still. Be silent. Know that God is near.*

PRAY

God heals the brokenhearted
and binds up their wounds.
God tells the number of the stars;
he calls each by name.

~*Psalm 147:3–4*

LISTEN

*Read Matthew 9:35–10:1, 5a, 6–8.*

At the sight of the crowds, Jesus' heart was moved
with pity for them, because they were troubled and
abandoned, like sheep without a shepherd.

~*Matthew 9:36*

## Don't Be a Mrs. Gadabout

*A Shepherd Looks at Psalm 23* is a book by modern-day
shepherd W. Phillip Keller. In the book, Keller recounts
the story of one of his prize ewes. She was one of his
most attractive sheep. Her body was beautifully pro-
portioned, and she had a strong constitution and an
excellent coat of wool. She was alert, with bright eyes,
and she bore sturdy lambs. But in spite of all these
excellent qualities, she had one distinct fault—she was
restless. Keller named her Mrs. Gadabout. No matter
what pasture she was in, she was always searching to
escape to greener pastures and, worse yet, she taught
her lambs to do the same. Like a good shepherd, Keller

always went to retrieve or rescue her from whatever trouble she got herself into, and he brought her back home.

Sometimes you may find yourself a little like Mrs. Gadabout—restless, troubled, and trying to escape. I know I do. It is easy to venture off the Gospel path of truth, simplicity, and love. We live in a world that constantly draws us away from God's path and tempts us with what seems to be an easier, more exciting, and glamorous life. We look to food, drink, money, or other material things to satisfy our inner emptiness. There is a Mrs. Gadabout in each of us. Sometimes we get in over our heads, but it is never too late, because we have a Savior who loves us unconditionally and desires to bring us back to the pasture of God's mercy and forgiveness. Jesus is the Good Shepherd who cares for each of his sheep and gently leads us back from emptiness to fullness, trouble to peace, abandonment to belonging.

## ACT

Identify someone you know who has strayed from God. Pray for the grace to show compassion for that person, and find a way to reach out to him or her today. What can you do to be God's loving presence?

## PRAY

Come, O Lord. Thank you for always searching for me, tending my wounds, and bringing me back home to you. Give me the grace to be a good shepherd to those entrusted to my care and to move beyond myself to help a neighbor in need. Amen.

# SUNDAY, DECEMBER 6
## SECOND WEEK OF ADVENT

BEGIN

*Be still. Be silent. Know that God is near.*

PRAY

The LORD has done great things for us; we are filled with joy!

*~See Psalm 126:3*

LISTEN

*Read Luke 3:1–6.*

John went throughout the whole region of the Jordan, proclaiming a baptism of repentance for the forgiveness of sins, as it is written in the book of the words of the prophet Isaiah: *A voice of one crying out in the desert: "Prepare the way of the Lord, make straight his paths."*

*~Luke 3:3–4*

## Let It Go and Start Again

It may be the catchy tune or the easy-to-remember lyrics that attract my grandniece Cadence (and so many other young children) to the hit song from *Frozen*, "Let It Go," but I think the message of being unburdened from our anger or shame or sinfulness is also captivating for us adults. "Let it go" can be a prayerful mantra for we who desire to be set free and start again this Advent as we prepare for Christmas and the ending of the year.

In the Advent scriptures, John the Baptist emerges from the wilderness shouting, not singing,

"Let it go." The letting go he proclaims begins with repentance. To repent means to turn, to stop going in one direction and instead go in another. It means to change, and we usually do not like people who tell us we need to change. The urging to let go of our vices, repent, and return to God's holy way is a constant in our lives.

John the Baptist prepares the way of the Lord, calling us to another way, a new way—the way of Jesus, the way of forgiveness. He pushes us out of the wilderness of hatred and condemnation, shouting, "Make straight the path!" "Prepare the way of the Lord!" It is a radical call to love, a call to change our way of thinking, living, and acting.

The glad tidings of joy celebrated at Christmas are in large part the announcement of God's forgiveness and mercy made flesh in the person of Jesus. Therefore, Advent preparation for Christmas involves repentance for our sins and reconciliation with God and with anyone in our lives with whom we are not in right relationship. Trust in God's mercy and let it go!

ACT

> Find out if and when your parish has a communal penance or reconciliation service or when confessions are scheduled. Go celebrate the sacrament. Embrace forgiveness.

PRAY

> Come, O Lord. Help me to be more willing to forgive so that I may know forgiveness and live in closer harmony with you, myself, and others. Amen.

# MONDAY, DECEMBER 7
## SECOND WEEK OF ADVENT

BEGIN

*Be still. Be silent. Know that God is near.*

PRAY

Strengthen hands that are feeble,
make firm the knees that are weak,
Say to those whose hearts are frightened:
Be strong, fear not! Here is your God.

*~Isaiah 35:3-4*

LISTEN

*Read Luke 5:17–26.*

And some men brought on a stretcher a man who
was paralyzed; they were trying to bring him in
and set him in Jesus' presence. But not finding a
way to bring him in because of the crowd, they
went up on the roof and lowered him on the
stretcher through the tiles and into the middle in
front of Jesus.

*~Luke 5:18–19*

## Carry a Friend to Jesus

Last year my sister Mary was diagnosed with breast
cancer. Mary, who puts nothing in her mouth that
isn't organic (except Snickers bars), was devastated.
Doug her faithful husband and soul mate, was equally
distraught. As Mary moved through the process of
choosing a surgeon and undergoing tests, a double
mastectomy, and a course of chemotherapy, there were
family, friends, neighbors, health practitioners, and
even strangers who carried her through each of these

difficult steps on her way to healing. A woman of deep faith, my sister got through the surgery with remarkable courage. But the prospect of chemotherapy paralyzed her with fear. Anxiety kept breaking through in spite of medication that should have helped. She shared her struggle with her small-faith community. They responded by gathering in Mary's home every Thursday evening before her chemo to pray with her. They and so many others carried Mary, paralyzed by fear, to the feet of Jesus.

In today's gospel reading, a group of friends and family brought a paralyzed man to Jesus. It was not an easy process. However, together they overcame every obstacle with conviction and creativity. There were those who prompted him to go to see Jesus to be healed, others carried him to the house, the group who cut open the roof, and those who lowered him into the midst of crowd, not to mention the householder who let his roof be cut open. It took a village of people to bring the paralyzed man to Jesus. Jesus responded to their loving actions by freeing him of both his sin and his paralysis.

We are called to bring one another to Jesus for physical, emotional, and spiritual healing. Yes, we need community.

ACT

Reach out to someone who is going through a health crisis with a visit, a call, or a simple meal.

PRAY

Come, O Lord. Extend your healing power upon my family, friends, and neighbors who are sick emotionally, physically, or spiritually. I place each of them before you by name. Amen.

# Tuesday, December 8

## Second Week of Advent
## Feast of the Immaculate Conception

BEGIN

*Be still. Be silent. Know that God is near.*

PRAY

Sing to the LORD a new song, for God has done wondrous deeds.

*~Psalm 98:1*

LISTEN

*Read Luke 1:26–38.*

And coming to Mary, the angel said, "Hail, full of grace! The Lord is with you." But she was greatly troubled at what was said and pondered what sort of greeting this might be. Then the angel said to her, "Do not be afraid, Mary, for you have found favor with God. Behold, you will conceive in your womb and bear a son, and you shall name him Jesus."

*~Luke 1:28–30*

## Cracked and Holy Vessels

Last Advent I visited the Philadelphia Museum of Art with two friends to view and pray with the painting *The Annunciation* by Henry Ossawa Tanner. Tanner, an American artist, painted this scene in 1898 after visiting the Holy Land. While there, he was deeply moved by his experience of painting ordinary Jewish people where Jesus lived and carried out his mission.

Many traditional European paintings of the annunciation depict Mary with a European face, wearing fancy blue robes and seated on a throne in a cathedral or palace. In contrast, Tanner paints Mary with authenticity and simplicity. He portrays her as a teenage girl, with olive skin, dressed in peasant clothes, sitting on a rumpled bed, and in a simple room. Today I am drawn to the three pottery vessels in the corners of the painting. They represent Mary, who will soon become the vessel of Jesus, the son of God and Mary.

Mary, favored by God in a unique way through her immaculate conception, becomes the spotless vessel for God's son. She is unflawed but vulnerable and fragile. In the painting, Mary is a bit troubled and anxious, but she freely accepts the grace given to her as she responds to God's messenger.

Meister Eckhart, a German Dominican mystic, wrote, "We are all meant to be mothers of God . . . for God always needs to be born." We, too, are called to be God's vessels and to be like Mary, God-bearers in our day and in our unique way. Like me, your vessel might be slightly cracked and a bit tarnished but ready and able through the power of God's gracious spirit to become vessels of God's amazing grace to those most in need.

ACT

Google Henry Ossawa Tanner's painting *The Annunciation*. Sit quietly and ponder it.

PRAY

Come, O Lord. Fashion me into a vessel of your love and mercy. Like Mary, help me to surrender my life into your hands. Amen.

# WEDNESDAY, DECEMBER 9
## SECOND WEEK OF ADVENT

BEGIN

*Be still. Be silent. Know that God is near.*

PRAY

They that hope in the LORD
will renew their strength,
they will soar as with eagle's wings;
they will run and not grow weary,
walk and not grow faint.

*~Isaiah 40:31*

LISTEN

*Read Matthew 11:28–30.*

Jesus said to the crowds: "Come to me, all you who
labor and are burdened, and I will give you rest.
Take my yoke upon you and learn from me, for I
am meek and humble of heart; and you will find
rest for yourselves. For my yoke is easy, and my
burden light."

*~Matthew 11:28–30*

## A Great Invitation

Preachers often explain the "yoke" in this passage as
the wooden instrument that yoked two oxen together
in Jesus' agricultural community. It is a metaphor
that lends itself to reflecting on how we don't have
to shoulder the yoke of life's burdens alone. As Jesus'
disciples, we know that he will share our yoke and
make our burdens, if not light, at least bearable.

Another possible interpretation is that the expres-
sion refers to the "yoke" of the rabbi. In Jesus' time,

each master rabbi had his own particular interpretation of the Torah (Jewish law), and that interpretation was called "his yoke." The disciples of the master rabbi would immerse themselves in the yoke of their rabbi—the teachings of their master. The yoke was heavy with law and tradition, and studying to become a rabbi was an arduous task reserved only for the best and brightest. Unlike other rabbis, Jesus did not wait for perfect disciples to come to him but instead called all who chose to follow his way of love. His interpretation of the Hebrew scriptures and rabbinical traditions was simpler and more compassionate—love God and love your neighbor, and all else will follow.

Today's great invitation to come to Jesus is for all who know themselves to be weighed down by life's troubles and in need of God's redeeming love. Jesus desires to free us from shame, guilt, judgment, and fear and lighten the burdens of our sufferings. It is an invitation to learn and become Jesus' disciples. We are not flawless, but we love God and want to follow his way. We will fall from time to time, but Jesus believes in us and the power of God's Spirit to transform us. He invites us to put on his yoke of mercy and to share his yoke of mercy with others.

ACT

Ask God today for grace to take on Jesus' yoke of love and mercy—to say yes to becoming a better disciple.

PRAY

Come, Lord Jesus. Help me to prepare my heart to more fully accept your love in my life. I say yes to being your disciple and to loving you and all those you have placed in my life. Amen.

BEGIN

*Be still. Be silent. Slowly repeat, "Come, O Lord."*

PRAY

The LORD is gracious and merciful; slow to anger, and of great kindness.

*~Psalm 145:8*

LISTEN

*Read Matthew 11:11–15.*

Jesus said to the crowds: "Amen, I say to you, there has been none greater than John the Baptist; yet the least in the kingdom of heaven is greater than he."

*~Matthew 11:11*

## *Pointing to Christ*

Eleven of my twenty grandnieces and grandnephews are under the age of three. I love being around them, and I delight in their fascination with the world. At around one year old, children begin to communicate by pointing. Child researchers have studied this very complex act. They report that children point for various reasons and that babies in particular point because they want to share their experience of the world. Babies point to things that delight or amaze them—like those Christmas lights that multiply as we get closer to Christmas. The desire to communicate is part of what makes us human.

While visiting St. John's Abbey in Collegeville, Minnesota, I was struck by a very poignant statue of

St. John the Baptist with his finger pointing—pointing to Christ. This finger pointing is not in a gesture of blame or judgment; instead, it is John wanting to share his experience of Christ with the world. His passionate witness to Christ is what makes John great.

John was great not because he was a strong and bold prophet but more importantly because he experienced Jesus as the Christ and pointed out that truth to his followers. John was able to step aside, let go of his ego, and guide his passionate followers away from him and toward Jesus. In today's gospel reading, Jesus addresses John's followers and tells them they will be as great as John the Baptist if they choose to enter the kingdom of God—to let go of all and follow the way of Christ.

We too are called to point others to Christ—to witness to our experiences of God's goodness and mercy. We give witness by sharing our experiences of God with humility and respect and, most importantly, through our charitable works and just acts.

ACT

Find one way to overtly witness your faith in Christ today. It might be as simple as a brief visit to church on your lunch break or wishing a store clerk a blessed day. It may be finding a way to talk about your faith at the office or telling a coworker you will pray for him or her.

PRAY

Come, O Lord. Give me the courage to share my faith story with others with humility and respect. Help me to bear witness to your presence by being a loving and forgiving person. Amen.

# FRIDAY, DECEMBER 11
## SECOND WEEK OF ADVENT

BEGIN

*Be still. Be silent. Know that God is near.*

PRAY

Those who follow you, Lord, will have the light of life.

*~See John 8:12*

LISTEN

*Read Matthew 11:16–19.*

Jesus said to the crowds: "To what should I compare this generation? It is like children who sit in marketplaces and call to one another, 'We played the flute for you, but you did not dance, we sang a dirge but you did not mourn.' For John came neither eating nor drinking, and they said, 'He is possessed by a demon.' The Son of Man came eating and drinking and they said, 'Look, he is a glutton and a drunkard, a friend of tax collectors and sinners.'"

*~Matthew 11:16–18a*

## *God, Speak to Me*

There is a story recounted in Sr. Anne Bryan Smollin's book *Live, Laugh, and Be Blessed* about a man who missed the many ways God was speaking to him:

The man whispered, "God, speak to me." And the meadow lark sang. But the man did not hear. So the man yelled, "God, speak to me." And thunder and lightning rolled across the sky. But the man did not listen. The man looked around and said, "God, let me see you." And a star shone brightly. But the man did not see. And the man shouted, "God, show me a miracle." And a life was born. But the man did not notice. So the man cried out in despair, "Touch me, God, and let me know you are here." Whereupon God reached down and touched the man. But the man brushed the butterfly away and walked on.

The crowd did not listen to the words of either the austere and fiery John the Baptist or the social and compassionate Jesus. They responded with neither the joy of dancing nor the empathy of mourning. The crowd rejected the words of these men of God who did not meet their expectations of a prophet or a savior. John seemed a bit too eccentric and weird, and Jesus was just too worldly—eating and drinking with sinners.

Sometimes God speaks to us through unexpected people and shows forth his presence in unlikely situations. Do you have the eyes to see God's unfolding presence and the ears to hear God speak through the people and events of your everyday life?

God speaks to us in his Word, the sacraments, creation, and in the stuff of our everyday lives. We often say prayers but spend little time in silence listening or watching in the darkness.

ACT

Take a walk outside and be attentive to the signs of God's presence in nature.

PRAY

Come, O Lord. O God, speak to me. O God, touch me. O God, let me see you in the events of my day. Amen.

# Saturday, December 12

## Second Week of Advent
## Feast of Our Lady of Guadalupe

BEGIN

*Be still. Be silent. Know that God is near.*

PRAY

Sing and rejoice, O daughter Zion!
See, I am coming to dwell among you, says the
LORD.

*~Zechariah 2:14*

LISTEN

*Read Luke 1:39–47.*

And Mary said:
"My soul proclaims the greatness of the Lord;
my spirit rejoices in God my savior."

*~Luke 1:46–47*

## *A Church for the Poor*

A number of years ago, I went to Mexico City for a wedding. The day before the celebration, a few of us made a pilgrimage to the Shrine of Our Lady of Guadalupe. Pilgrims have been visiting this holy site since 1531. As I walked into the ancient basilica, I was moved by its beauty, the throngs of faith-filled people in prayer, and mostly by God's palpable presence among us.

Our Lady appeared on this site to a poor native, Juan Diego. She asked him to be her messenger and told him to go to the bishop and ask that a church be built on this site, where she could listen to the sufferings of the people and heal their wounds. She also told him to tell the bishop to make the care of Juan Diego's people a priority. Juan and his people were oppressed and marginalized, as she was. The bishop was skeptical and asked Juan for a sign. Juan returned to the hillside and Our Lady gave him a cloak full of beautiful roses that miraculously bloomed on the spot.

When Juan opened his *tilma* (cloak) to show the bishop the sign of these rare roses, Mary's sacred image was imprinted there. The *tilma* is venerated at the basilica this day. It is a sign of God's unconditional love for people of all races and colors, for the poor and disenfranchised, and is a sign of each person's dignity before God.

At the end of today's gospel reading, Mary begins her Magnificat with rejoicing in God. She praises a God who denounces those who disregard the poor and a God who lifts up the lowly and fills the hungry with good things. She becomes the voice for all the suffering, and she promises God's mercy to them. Our Lady of Guadalupe challenges us to care for those in most need. In her voice, I hear the challenge of Pope Francis: "How I would like a church that is poor and for the poor."

ACT

Instead of exchanging gifts with colleagues, friends, or even family this Christmas, suggest that instead you give to a local outreach center.

PRAY

Come, O Lord. Give me a heart for people who are poor and suffering. Help me give generously to the stranger. Amen.

# Sunday, December 13
## Third Week of Advent

BEGIN

*Be still. Be silent. Know that God is near.*

PRAY

Have no anxiety at all, but in everything, by
prayer and petition, with thanksgiving, make your
requests known to God.

*~Philippians 4:6*

LISTEN

*Read Luke 3:10–18.*

The crowds asked John the Baptist, "What should
we do?" He said to them in reply, "Whoever has
two cloaks should share with the person who has
none. And whoever has food should do likewise.
Tax collectors . . . stop collecting more than what is
prescribed. Soldiers . . . do not practice extortion,
do not falsely accuse anyone, and be satisfied with
your wages."

*~Luke 3:10–11, 14*

## What Should We Do?

My friend Sally shared an experience she had many
years ago while volunteering at a Catholic Worker
soup kitchen in New York City. As she was serving the
soup, she heard an abrupt voice calling to her, "Hey
you, serving the soup, come here." It was Dorothy
Day, the founder of the Catholic Worker. She said to
Sally, "What do you think you are doing, serving the
soup like this and looking at the people with disgust?"
And then, with a softer tone she said, "Don't you

know that each of us is broken in some way? For some of us, the brokenness is shown on the outside, but for others it is hidden deep inside. You first have to look at your own brokenness before you can understand someone else's. It is only then that you will truly share a meal with the homeless." Dorothy Day continued, "Just picture all those broken pieces coming together and forming a beautiful mosaic." Then in a loud deep voice, she said, "Now please go, and don't return until you can see that mosaic, first in yourself and then in every person you meet, including the homeless and unwanted." Sally's encounter with Dorothy Day was a difficult but life-changing experience.

Dorothy Day, like John the Baptist, was a prophetic preacher—preparing the way of the Lord. For Dorothy Day, it wasn't enough to simply donate money or volunteer to help the poor. Christians must do more. John the Baptist did not require the soldier and tax collector to change their professions but to make changes in their attitudes toward their daily work.

How then shall we prepare the way of the Lord? What shall we do?

ACT

Today, give careful consideration to where you can encounter the mosaic Dorothy Day talked about. Make a plan to go there and immerse yourself in whatever service is needed.

PRAY

Come, O Lord. Grace me with a heart of mercy and care and a spirit of committed love that knows how to share itself. Amen.

# Monday, December 14
## Third Week of Advent

BEGIN

*Be still. Be silent. Know that God is near.*

PRAY

Your ways, O Lord, make known to me;
teach me your paths,
Guide me in your truth and teach me,
for you are God my Savior.

*~Psalm 25:4–5*

LISTEN

*Read Matthew 21:23–27.*

When Jesus had come into the temple area, the chief priests and the elders of the people approached him as he was teaching and said, "By what authority are you doing these things? And who gave you this authority?"

*~Matthew 21:23*

### *Authority Comes from Within*

A number of years ago, I was sharing with my spiritual director for the umpteenth time about an ongoing struggle to make a decision—it was a choice between two goods. Her response to me was, "No decision is a decision." I think I wanted her to tell me what to do. Of course, as a good spiritual director she would not. Be careful of people who tell you what to do! They do not help you claim your inner authority and exercise the power God has given you to make decisions. In the New Testament, the Greek word for "authority" is *exousia,* which is often translated as "power." We need to recognize that power in ourselves.

Many of us suffer from poor self-esteem and thus doubt our own inner power and authority. We are constantly looking for validation from others. We hesitate to state what we believe in our hearts for fear of being judged or, worse, rejected. It becomes more complicated when people in authority tell us to do something that we know in our hearts is not right. In today's gospel reading, Jesus' authority is questioned by the religious officials of his day. Jesus does not back down. He instead trusts in the power of God's spirit within to guide him.

We too have the power of God within us, and we need to trust the Holy Spirit to guide us.

Exerting personal authority means taking responsibility for the consequences of our choices and working hard to change what is not working instead of blaming and complaining. Have courage, face your fears, and take action. Trust in the power of God within to do the right thing. If later you find you made a wrong choice, admit it and use your resources to make it right.

## ACT

Name one decision you made this year that did not go the way you wanted. Don't blame or complain. Instead, take responsibility for the consequences of that choice. Use all your God-given resources to change what isn't working.

## PRAY

Come, O Lord. Make your ways known to me, and teach me your path. Help me to trust in myself and the power of your Spirit within me. Amen.

# Tuesday, December 15
## Third Week of Advent

BEGIN

*Be still. Be silent. Know that God is near.*

PRAY

The Lord is close to the brokenhearted; and those who are crushed in spirit God saves.

*~Psalm 34:18*

LISTEN

*Read Matthew 21:28–32.*

A man had two sons. He came to the first and said, "Son, go out and work in the vineyard today." The son said in reply, "I will not," but afterward he changed his mind and went. The man came to the other son and gave the same order. He said in reply, "Yes, sir," but did not go.

*~Matthew 21:28–30*

## Get off the Couch!

Last year, toward the end of the Advent season, Pope Francis gave his traditional pre-Christmas greetings to the Roman Curia (the central governing body of the universal Church). He invited his colleagues and collaborators to examine their consciences and to prepare for the Sacrament of Reconciliation as a way to ready their hearts for Christmas. The crowd, composed mostly of cardinals, did not look happy. Pope Francis boldly listed fifteen "diseases" that he saw present in the Curia and explored each one in detail. He mentioned vainglory and feeling overly important, "spiritual Alzheimer's" and hoarding money and power. He spoke of cliques and concern for worldly profit as well as the "terrorism of gossip." Pope Francis explained that these "diseases" and "temptations" do not concern only the Curia but "are naturally a danger to every Christian and every curia, community, congregation, parish, and ecclesiastic movement." And I would add any family or business.

In today's gospel, Jesus told the poignant story of the two sons in the vineyard in order to convey a strong message primarily directed at the chief priests and religious leaders of his day. They, like the cardinals, were not happy that this message was directed at them.

Praying daily and going to Mass on Sunday is not enough. It is time for us to get off the couch to answer the knock at the door and let our hurting neighbors into our lives. Advent is a prime time for us to answer the pope's challenge to undertake an examination of conscience, ask for forgiveness for our sins of both commission and omission, and prepare our hearts to receive Christ anew.

ACT

This week, examine your conscience. Have you engaged in: gossip, forming cliques, abusing money or power, arrogance, or forgetting about God and the needs of the poor?

PRAY

Come, O Lord. Open my heart to your mercy and forgiveness. Amen.

# WEDNESDAY, DECEMBER 16
## THIRD WEEK OF ADVENT

BEGIN

*Be still. Be silent. Know that God is near.*

PRAY

Kindness and truth shall meet;
justice and peace shall kiss.
Truth shall spring out of the earth,
and justice shall look down from heaven.

*~Psalm 85:11–12*

LISTEN

*Read Luke 7:18b–23.*

And Jesus said to them in reply, "Go and tell John
what you have seen and heard: the blind regain
their sight, the lame walk, lepers are cleansed, the
deaf hear, and the dead are raised, the poor have
the good news proclaimed to them. And blessed is
the one who takes no offense at me."

*~Luke 7:22–23*

## *Evidence Enough to Convict You?*

If you were arrested for being a Christian, would there
be enough evidence to convict you? Martin Niemöller,
a Protestant pastor who resisted the Nazi regime in
Germany, is cited as the author of this quotation:

In Germany, they came first for the communists,
And I didn't speak up because I wasn't a commu-
nist. When they locked up the social democrats,
I remained silent; I was not a social democrat . . .
then they came for the Jews, And I didn't speak up

because I wasn't a Jew . . . When they came for me,
there was no one left to speak out.

John the Baptist sent two of his disciples to ask Jesus,
"Are you the one to come or should we look for
another?" Jesus' response to that question was not a
carefully stated case of how he was the fulfillment of
the messianic prophesies in the Hebrew scriptures.
Nor was his response a display of his mastery of the
Torah or a declaration of his strict adherence to Jewish
worship and ritual. He simply replied, in effect, "Look
at my actions; they speak for themselves." After hear-
ing this, John knew that Jesus was the Messiah.

Jesus' works of mercy in his healing, forgiving,
and preaching good news to the poor were a powerful testimony to his true identity, and they led to his
crucifixion. Sometimes when you are doing the work
of God people may accuse you of being a revolution-
ary or a naive do-gooder. If you are never questioned
or criticized for doing God's work, you may have to
wonder if it is really God's work.

ACT

Identify one injustice that you encounter almost
every day but tend to overlook complacently.
Today, change your response. Take a stand against
the wrong.

PRAY

Come, O Lord. Give me the courage to stand up for
what is right and to defend those who are scorned
because of their beliefs. Amen.

# Thursday, December 17
## Third Week of Advent

*In* The Liturgy of the Hours *today, we begin the "O Antiphons," which are recited before the "Magnificat" during Evening Prayer and—in a different translation and slightly different order—as the alleluia verses for Mass during the same period. Each of the "O Antiphons" begins by invoking one of the titles of the Messiah from the prophecy of Isaiah—a prophecy fulfilled in the birth of Jesus.*

BEGIN

*Be still. Be silent. Know that God is near.*

PRAY

O Wisdom of God Most High, guiding creation with power and love: come to teach us the path of truth and knowledge.

*~O Antiphon*

LISTEN

*Read Matthew 1:1–17.*

The book of the genealogy of Jesus Christ, son of David, the son of Abraham. Abraham became the father of Isaac, Isaac the father of Jacob, Jacob the father of Judah and his brothers. Judah became the father of Perez and Zerah. Whose mother was Tamar . . . Eleazar became the father of Matthan, Matthan the father of Jacob, Jacob the father of Joseph, the husband of Mary. Of her was born Jesus who is called the Christ."

*~Matthew 1:1–3a, 15–16*

## Ordinary and Extraordinary Ways

My brother Joe has been investigating our family tree with the same intensity and enthusiasm he invests in all things that interest him. His wife, ever gracious, has visited more upstate New York cemeteries searching for dead Rickards than she cares to remember. Joe claims that when he is finished with his research he will write a book titled *How the Rickards Saved America*. We tease my brother, but his findings are interesting, and they add to our colorful family narrative.

Jesus' genealogy affirms his humanity, embodied in a series of unique names representing persons, small and great, known and unknown, saints and sinners, women and men from all nations. Some of the persons listed have colorful stories involving questionable sexual and unethical behavior. God works through ordinary and even scandalous human beings.

Each of us has a family tree; if you shake it hard enough, more than a few nuts will fall out. But these nuts are part of our history and our identity, and God has worked through each of them to bring us to faith. The God who acted through ordinary, imperfect human beings to bring Jesus to the world is the same God who acts in our own families in ordinary and extraordinary ways.

ACT

Pray for one of your family members with whom you have particular difficulty; ask God for the grace to accept and forgive that person.

PRAY

Come, Wisdom of God. Help me to understand, accept, and love my family with all our imperfections. Teach me gratitude for the ordinary. Amen.

# Friday, December 18

## Third Week of Advent

BEGIN

*Be still. Be silent. Know that God is near.*

PRAY

O Adonai, O Leader of the House of Israel: come to rule your people with justice!

*~O Antiphon*

LISTEN

*Read Matthew 1:18–25.*

[B]ehold, the angel of the Lord appeared to Joseph in a dream and said, "Joseph, son of David, do not be afraid to take Mary your wife into your home. For it is through the Holy Spirit that this child has been conceived in her. She will bear a son and name him Jesus, because he will save his people from their sins." When Joseph awoke, he did what the angel commanded him.

*~Matthew 1:20–21, 24*

### St. Joseph, a Model Disciple

The convent where I now live was previously home to a community of the Sisters of St. Joseph. We Dominicans moved in and quickly began to make the convent our home by putting up pictures of our Dominican saints—Dominic, Catherine of Siena, and Martin de Porres. One of the pictures the other sisters left behind, and we left hanging, is a touching yet unusual picture of a young St. Joseph, painted as an ordinary man of his day, tenderly holding the baby Jesus. Visitors who notice the picture often ask, "Who is that?"

Joseph, usually in the background of the Nativity story, stands at the beginning of Matthew's gospel as a model of discipleship. The scripture tells us he was a righteous or just man. He finds himself in a moral dilemma—he wants to show mercy to Mary and not expose her disgrace, and yet he must obey the Jewish Law by not accepting what might appear to be adultery. His difficult inner deliberations are cut short by divine intervention—an angel appears to Joseph in a dream and asks him to set aside his previous understanding of God's will and to marry Mary, a pregnant woman. Joseph, being just, obeys God's command immediately and adopts Jesus as his son. Joseph had a compassionate and forgiving heart and was able to put aside his ego and accept Mary as his wife. His heart was not hardened by judgment or revenge or fear of what others may say. He was not stuck on the letter of the law, and he was thus able to hear God's voice.

Sometimes we find ourselves in a moral dilemma—condemnation or mercy? Do we judge another by the letter of the law, or is there room in our deliberations for mercy?

ACT

Think of someone whom you have judged or even cut off from your life because of some wrong you have seen that person do. Today, take one step toward mending that realtionship.

PRAY

Come, O Adonai, leader of the just and merciful. Open my heart to your compassionate word, and fill me with your mercy. Amen.

# Saturday, December 19

## Third Week of Advent

BEGIN

*Be still. Be silent. Know that God is near.*

PRAY

O Root of Jesse's stem, flower of God's love: come
and refresh us with the fragrance of your glory.

*~O Antiphon*

LISTEN

*Read Luke 1:5–25.*

But the angel said to him, "Do not be afraid, Zechariah, because your prayers have been heard. Your
wife Elizabeth will bear a son, and you shall name
him John." . . . Then Zechariah said to the angel,
"How shall I know this? For I am old man, and my
wife is advanced in years."

*~Luke 1:13, 18*

## *All Is Possible with God*

I was out jogging one day after Hurricane Sandy,
which had devastated New Jersey and other states in
the Northeast in the fall of 2012. I was having difficulty
navigating around all the felled trees. Some were very
old and stately trees, now broken and dead, waiting to
be carted away. It was a sad scene, very like a grave-
yard. The following spring, I was out jogging again
on that same path, and I noticed to my delight one of
the remaining old stumps with the tiniest green shoot
poking out through its tough old skin. This new shoot
proclaimed symbolically the very same message that

would eventually become clear to the tired old Zechariah: all is possible with God.

Zechariah, an elderly and faithful priest, was praying fervently but still surprised when God answered his prayer. He was offering incense in the Holy of Holies, the temple sanctuary in which Jews believed God was immanently present. Even still, he did not expect to encounter the powerful presence of his God. He was amazed that his longstanding prayer had been answered. The revelation about two old bodies bringing forth a lively new baby seemed impossible.

This gospel scene challenges us to trust that God is truly present—not only in sanctuaries and not only in times of prayer, but always and everywhere—and that God hears our prayers. We can go through the motions of prayer and worship, but we truly have faith only if we expect to encounter God, both while we are at worship and in our daily activities. Advent is a time to be renewed in our faith and in the belief that God is with us and that, with God, all things are indeed possible.

ACT

> Write down at least one area of your life in which you believe you have grown old or stale. Then write a brief prayer asking God to bring new life there. Pray your prayer each day from now until Christmas.

PRAY

> Come, Root of Jesse. Bring forth new life in the areas of my life that have become old or stale. Amen.

# SUNDAY, DECEMBER 20
## FOURTH WEEK OF ADVENT

BEGIN

*Be still. Be silent. Know that God is near.*

PRAY

O Key of David, open the gates of God's eternal realm, come and free the prisoners of darkness.

*~O Antiphon*

LISTEN

*Read Luke 1:39–45.*

When Elizabeth heard Mary's greeting, the infant leaped in her womb, and Elizabeth, filled with the Holy Spirit, cried out in a loud voice and said, "Most blessed are you among women, and blessed is the fruit of your womb."

*~Luke 1:41–42*

## Visitation Events

Have you ever had someone show up in your life just in time to get you through a difficult or painful event? These are "visitation events," in which God sends a messenger of his love and an angel of grace to accompany you. Sometimes these "angels" are well-known friends and family members; other times they are complete strangers.

In today's gospel story, Mary, a young woman, goes to visit her older cousin, Elizabeth, when both women are in the midst of unexpected pregnancies. We don't know anything about their relationship prior to this event. Maybe Elizabeth helped care for Mary when Mary was a child, or perhaps Mary's mom asked Mary to go to help Elizabeth. Or perhaps, in light of the awkward situation, Mary's family just wanted to get her out of town. Whatever the case, we know from the scriptures that Mary, fresh from her encounter with the angel, went "in haste" to visit Elizabeth. This journey was a courageous act in itself. In Mary's time, travel for other than customary reasons was outside the norm. While a journey to visit family was legitimate, Mary's sojourn alone to the "hill country" would have been highly unusual and improper. Yet Mary goes to visit her cousin.

As we approach Christmas, many of us receive visitors and go to visit loved ones. Think of these occasions as visitation events in which, through your love and good cheer, you can make God present to your friends and families. Let your visiting herald good news. The greatest gifts we can give one another are time and presence. Let go of all the unrealistic expectations that come with the Christmas season, and enjoy the simple beauty of visiting.

ACT

Visit someone today whom you haven't planned to: perhaps a coworker for a quick hello and a kind word or a neighbor for a Christmas greeting. Or arrange a visit with someone who may be alone this Christmas season.

PRAY

Come, O Key of David. Open my heart to the visitors you send me. Help me to be, like Mary, a Christ-bearer to whatever home I enter. Amen.

# MONDAY, DECEMBER 21
## FOURTH WEEK OF ADVENT

*The gospel reading used here is from December 20
in the* Lectionary, *to avoid duplicating yesterday's
reading.*

BEGIN

*Be still. Be silent. Know that God is near.*

PRAY

O Radiant Dawn, splendor of eternal light, sun
of justice, come and shine on those who dwell in
darkness.

*~O Antiphons*

LISTEN

*Read Luke 1:26–38.*

Then the angel said to her, "Do not be afraid, Mary,
for you have found favor with God. Behold, you
will conceive in your womb and bear a son, and
you shall name him Jesus."

*~Luke 1:30–31*

## Waiting in the Darkness

Today, December 21, is the winter solstice, the darkest
day of the year here in the northern hemisphere. It is
the day of least light, as the sun is at its lowest point.
Our ancient ancestors were gripped with fear and anxiety on this day, wondering whether the sun would
reverse its descent and move back up in the sky. Each
year they would wait in darkness and fear, only to dis-
cover inevitably that the sun would be "reborn" and
begin its ascent once again. Every ancient civilization

celebrated the rebirth of the sun. Fear became trust as life continued and light once again overcame the darkness.

Advent is a time of waiting; as the winter solstice reminds us, sometimes it means waiting in darkness. The angel said to Mary, "Do not be afraid." Her anxiety and doubt must have been evident, yet she trusted, and she waited. Our God dwells in deep darkness as well as in bright light. I always envision the angel Gabriel coming to Mary at night, and there are other places in scripture where God comes to people in dark clouds and dark dreams. At the darkest time, near the darkest day of the year, Mary gave birth to Jesus, the light of the world. God comes to us during those long restless nights, beside a hospice bed, in the struggle to overcome an addiction, in the dark room of shame and self-hatred.

We all experience dark times; no one who is human gets to skip the dark cloud. At times it feels as if the light will never come and that God has abandoned us. We are afraid, doubtful, and tired. Even still, we trust and seek God in the darkness while we wait for the light.

ACT

Recall a dark time when you encountered God. Even though you would have never chosen it, what were the blessings?

PRAY

Come, Radiant Dawn! Help me to seek you in the darkness and find my way through your grace into the light. Amen.

# TUESDAY, DECEMBER 22
## FOURTH WEEK OF ADVENT

BEGIN

*Be still. Be silent. Know that God is near.*

PRAY

O Desire of Nations and Keystone of the Church,
come, O Promised One, and bring us peace!

*~O Antiphons*

LISTEN

*Read Luke 1:46–56.*

Mary said,
"My soul proclaims the greatness of the Lord;
my spirit rejoices in God my savior.
For he has looked upon his lowly servant.
From this day all generations will call me blessed:
the Almighty has done great things for me, and
Holy is his name!"

*~Luke 1:46–49*

## The God of the Unexpected

My nephew Tom and his wife Amy were married
for fifteen years. They longed for a child. After many
years and numerous miscarriages, they had given up
hope and began to pray to accept their situation. At
thirty-eight years of age, Amy discovered she was
pregnant again. She and Tom were more terrified
than delighted. They feared the worst. The doctor
advised Amy to stop working and to rest. Amy was
teaching, and she went to the home of one of her older
colleagues to seek her advice. The woman, to Amy's

surprise, said, "Let's pray about it." This was not what Amy had expected. They sat in the woman's living room, and they prayed. That period of spontaneous and heartfelt prayer deeply touched Amy's heart and opened her to a powerful and unexpected experience of God's presence. She knew all would be well. She and Tom returned to regularly participating in Mass, and they prayed with a new hope and confidence.

The scripture passage that spoke to Amy during her pregnancy was today's first reading, the story of Hannah. Hannah too longed for a child and prayed persistently for many years. God finally answered her prayer. Amy prayed with that reading many times during her pregnancy and gave birth to a beautiful baby boy, Thomas Aurelio. Many people attended Thomas's baptism; a huge party followed, with all of us rejoicing, for God had done great things for Tom and Amy and for all of us who love them.

Mary rejoiced in all God had done for her in both the expected and unexpected. God continues to bless our lives and do great things for us. Thank you, Lord, for the gift of life!

ACT

Pray today for a couple who is having difficulty conceiving a child—a couple you know or all couples facing this challenge.

PRAY

Come, Desire of Nations and Keystone of the Church. Open us to the unexpected and the surprising turns of your will. Amen.

# WEDNESDAY, DECEMBER 23
## FOURTH WEEK OF ADVENT

BEGIN

*Be still. Be silent. Know that God is near.*

PRAY

O Emmanuel, God-with-us, come to save us.

*~O Antiphons*

LISTEN

*Read Luke 1:57–66.*

"John is his name," and all were amazed. Immediately his mouth was opened, his tongue freed, and he spoke blessing God.

*~Luke 1:63b–64*

## Out of the Silence

A couple of years ago, I became aware that my voice was hoarse. I thought it must be from all the talking I do; my friends and family readily agreed! However, as the months went on, my voice grew hoarser. I finally decided to have my throat checked. My doctor, told me it was probably caused from straining my voice through preaching and public speaking. But to his surprise and my shock, he found a lesion on my right vocal cord, and he suspected cancer. You can guess what followed—feeling overwhelmed by the "c" word, a cacophony of advice from all interested parties, more tests, two biopsies, a second opinion, an obsessive Internet search, and finally surgery.

    After surgery, I had to be silent for a week—that in itself required divine intervention. The surgeon told me she hoped to save my voice, but she could not guarantee its quality. So I waited in silence. Would I, a member of the Dominicans, the Order of Preachers, be a preacher who could not be heard clearly or even speak at all? I vividly remember the day I was allowed to speak—out came my voice, a bit hoarse, but it sounded like me. I, like Zechariah in today's gospel reading, spoke blessing to God.

Earlier in this gospel story, Zechariah was silenced by God for questioning the possibility that his elderly wife, Elizabeth, could be pregnant. Zechariah, this poor old priest, was transformed into a most potent negative sign, a priest who could not speak, who could no longer offer prayers. His period of forced silence did not make Zechariah bitter but deepened his faith in the God who is gracious (the meaning of the name John). When his voice returned, he uttered blessings.

The period before and after my throat surgery was a dark time, a vulnerable time, but the silence was a place where God came to me. As the poet Tagore reminds us, "God comes, every moment and every age, every day and every night."

ACT

Today, spend twenty minutes in silence. Just sit and think or pray. Be still.

PRAY

Come, O Emmanuel, God-with-us. Come to save us. Amen.

# THURSDAY, DECEMBER 24
## CHRISTMAS EVE

BEGIN

*Be still. Be silent. Know that God is near.*

PRAY

The people who walked in darkness have seen a great light; upon those who dwelt in the land of gloom a light has shone.

*~Isaiah 9:1*

LISTEN

*Read Luke 2:1–14.*

The angel said to them, "Do not be afraid; for behold, I proclaim to you good news of great joy that will be for all the people. For today in the city of David a savior has been born for you who is Christ the Lord."

*~Luke 2:10–11*

## Christmas within Us

Fr. Joseph Healey tells this story in his book *Once Upon a Time in Africa.*

It was the night before Christmas in Africa, and an eight-year-old boy from Ghana was devastated because his village had been destroyed by the so-called army of liberation. He felt none of the usual joy and anticipation of the season. His parents had been killed, and many of his friends were kidnapped and never returned. In years past, Christmas in his village had always been a joyous festival with music, houses decorated with paper ornaments created by the children, roads filled with people visiting friends and relatives, and plentiful food and drink. The little boy wondered how Christmas could come without his parents and his village. How could he celebrate the birth of the Prince of Peace since he had not known any peace, only war and suffering?

As the boy continued to think about Christmases past and about the present suffering, he heard the horn of a car. It was a group of travelers who had taken a detour through his village, because the bridge over the river had been destroyed. They shared their food with the villagers and helped build a fire in the marketplace to keep the people warm.

The young boy's oldest sister was pregnant. She had not spoken since they had escaped the soldiers and was still in shock. She went into labor, and villagers and visitors removed their shirts to make a bed for her next to the fire. She gave birth to a beautiful boy. War or no war, they danced and sang Christmas carols until dawn. When the young mother was asked what she would name the baby, she spoke for the first time since the village had been destroyed. She said, "His name is *Gye Nyame*," which means "except God I fear none." And they celebrated Christmas that night.

ACT

Name at least one reason to hope, and share that hope with someone on Christmas day.

PRAY

O Christ, God among us, fill me with renewed hope and joy this day. Amen.

# Friday, December 25
## The Nativity of the Lord

BEGIN

*Be still. Be silent. Know that God is near.*

PRAY

How beautiful upon the mountains
are the feet of the one who brings glad tidings.

*~Isaiah 52:7a*

LISTEN

*Read John 1:1–18.*

And the Word became flesh and made his dwelling
among us, and we saw his glory, the glory of the
Father's only Son, full of grace and truth.

*~John 1:14*

## *Our God Is One with Us*

Last year, I read in the news a Christmas story about
a man named Jim Hipp, who is Santa for the annual
Christmas party in the burn unit of Akron Children's
Hospital. Jim is a unique Santa: he is a burn survivor.
Fifteen years ago, he was treated at this same hospital
for severe burns from an accident he endured while
working as an industrial engineer. Ten years ago, he
decided to give back by playing Santa at the hospital's annual party. According to the news account, the
children have embraced him with open arms. Hipp
remarked, "They say, 'Oh look, he's hurt too,' and they
will touch my face." "Why do you have scars? Have
you been burned?" they ask. Hipp replies, "Ho, Ho,
Ho. . . . Those chimneys can be very hot." Jim is an

especially powerful Santa for these children, because he is one with them—he bears the same kinds of scars and brings them joy.

Jesus, who is born among us, is fully God and fully one of us. We do not have a distant God but a personal God who loves us unconditionally, bears our scars, and lives among us. The incredible good news of this day is that the child born among us can be born again and again in those who believe. When we give of ourselves as Jesus did, then the goodness of God is revealed, and the glory of Jesus is made manifest. The Word then becomes flesh and makes his dwelling among us, and all will see God's glory.

## PRAYER FOR CHRISTMAS

Gracious God, we thank you for this Christmas day, for the gift of faith, family, and friends. Give us hearts grateful for the gifts we have received, the good food we are about to eat, and, most importantly, the birth of Jesus, born in our hearts this year. Fill us with joy this day, knowing God's personal and unconditional love for each of us as we try to follow the way of Jesus more closely— praying daily, loving deeply, forgiving frequently, and giving thanks always. Bless our family, those who spend Christmas alone, and families around the world who have no home or have little food to share this day. And bless our abundant food, those who prepared this meal, and each person around our table. We ask this through Jesus Christ, the God who lives among us. Amen.

**Theresa Rickard, O.P.,** is a Dominican Sister of Blauvelt, New York, and serves as the president and executive director of RENEW International. She earned a doctorate of ministry in preaching degree from Aquinas Institute of Theology in St. Louis, Missouri. Additionally, she earned a master of divinity degree at Union Theological Seminary in New York City and a master of arts in religion and religious education degree at Fordham University.

Since becoming executive director in 2007, Rickard has led RENEW International's expansion into more than forty dioceses in the United States, in parishes and on campuses, as well as into five developing countries.

# AVE

AVE MARIA PRESS

Founded in 1865, Ave Maria Press,
a ministry of the Congregation of
Holy Cross, is a Catholic publishing
company that serves the spiritual and
formative needs of the Church and its
schools, institutions, and ministers;
Christian individuals and families; and
others seeking spiritual nourishment.

For a complete listing of titles from

Ave Maria Press

Sorin Books

Forest of Peace

Christian Classics

visit www.avemariapress.com

AVE MARIA PRESS
Notre Dame, IN
A Ministry of the United States Province of Holy Cross